This address, dealing with the history of Lawrence Institute of Technology, was delivered at a "1985 Michigan Meeting" of The Newcomen Society of the United States held in Southfield, when Dr. Richard E. Marburger was the guest of honor and speaker on June 6th, 1985.

"At Lawrence Tech, our institution is the lengthened shadow of thousands of students and alumni: students who, in general, are different from those at other institutions— students who are intent upon turning ideas into reality."

—Dr. Richard E. Marburger

Lawrence Institute
of Technology

A Tale of Three Students

RICHARD E. MARBURGER, PH. D.

MEMBER OF THE NEWCOMEN SOCIETY

PRESIDENT

LAWRENCE INSTITUTE OF TECHNOLOGY

SOUTHFIELD, MICHIGAN

THE NEWCOMEN SOCIETY OF THE UNITED STATES

NEW YORK   EXTON   PRINCETON   PORTLAND

1985

Newcomen Publication Number 1248

Copyright, 1985
LAWRENCE INSTITUTE OF TECHNOLOGY

Library of Congress
Catalog Card Number 86-60104

Permission to abstract is granted
provided proper credit is allowed

The Newcomen Society, as a body,
is not responsible for opinions
expressed in the following pages

First Printing: June 1986

Fellow members of Newcomen and guests:

THE WITTY remark of George Bernard Shaw, "Those who can, do—and those who cannot, teach," has been applied to university professors. My colleague at Johns Hopkins University added, "Those who cannot teach—become university presidents!"

Richard Marburger is a major exception. He has been highly successful as a research engineer, as a university professor, and as the president of Lawrence Institute of Technology.

He was born both brilliant and exuberant. He brought honor to the Grace Evangelical Lutheran Parochial School in 1942 by winning the spelling bee against regional competition. He was an honor student at Kenyon College for two years before he transferred to Wayne State. There he won top honors for three degrees—B.S., M.A. and Ph.D. He was a research engineer with General Motors, then a professor at LIT, then a dean of the faculty. In academic circles, a dean of the faculty is generally defined as a mouse studying to be a rat! Marburger had no aspiration for power. He merely wished to serve.

That great and good academic genius, Wayne Buell, handpicked Richard Marburger to be the president of LIT. In this capacity, he has lifted this university to a place of greatness and distinction.

While the universities of America are stained with red ink, Richard Marburger has produced a surplus in excess of a quarter of a million dollars each year he has served as president of LIT. I know of no other institution of higher learning in America that can match this fiscal record.

Most of my colleagues who administer institutions of higher learning complain of academic fatigue. Richard Marburger is a veritable ball of fire! His disciplined energy appears to be boundless. He is in his office at the crack of dawn and stays as late as the exigencies require.

He is a great communicator. He knows how to deal with people. He has utilized all advanced technical equipment to facilitate communication. His system of computers, appropriate to a technological college, gives immediate access to each dean, each teacher, and to each of his university colleagues, as well as to the members of his board.

No wonder he has become a sort of celebrity—past president of the Engineering Society of Detroit—Gold Medal, Affiliate Council of that Society—The Horace H. Rackham Award. Recently, he went to New York to receive the Leadership Award of the American Society of Mechanical Engineers. He is a director of the Economic Club of Detroit.

Plato defined a great teacher as one who "holds before the young a vision of greatness." It is my pleasure to introduce a great teacher and our honored guest and speaker, RICHARD E. MARBURGER.

Fellow members of Newcomen and guests:

ACTORUM Memores simul affectamus Agenda—memories of acts in the past in similar fashion affect those things which are to come. This is the motto of The Newcomen Society and a statement which applies to Lawrence Institute of Technology with unrivalled appropriateness.

The great American philosopher, Ralph Waldo Emerson, once commented: "An institution is the lengthened shadow of one man."

At Lawrence Tech, our institution is the lengthened shadow of thousands of students and alumni: students who, in general, are different from those at other institutions—students who are intent upon turning ideas into reality.

This college is celebrating its thirtieth year in Southfield and its fifty-third year of existence. During those years, much has been learned about providing an excellent education at an affordable cost to those many students and alumni. It is of surpassing importance that we retain an understanding of the "acts of the past" which have enabled us to do that and to continue to understand what it is in the nature of our particular type of student that provides them with the extraordinary motivation and flair for turning ideas into reality that is their hallmark.

What, then, is our mechanism for usefully applying "memories of acts of the past" to current decision-making?

At this point, I am honored to request that the trustees and the members of the Corporation of Lawrence Institute of Technology who are present here tonight rise to be recognized! Collectively, they comprise the engine that drives this college. These steely-eyed but friendly people are the folks with the long memories. Two of them, Ben Bregi and Kurt Tech, are alumni. Judgment is the crucially important ingredient that the members and trustees apply.

Among the "acts of the past" which they continue to enshrine are concepts such as "the pay-as-you-go, no frills college" which optimizes the use of its resources and "does it right the first time." Adherence to these principles leads to fulfillment of our mission "an excellent education at an affordable cost."

Other important concepts which have stood the test of time include

LAWRENCE INSTITUTE OF TECHNOLOGY CELEBRATES THIRTY YEARS IN THE CITY OF
SOUTHFIELD DURING 1985. LIT'S MODERN, NINETY-ACRE CAMPUS IS WITHIN A FEW
MILES OF A NUMBER OF *FORTUNE* 500 COMPANY WORLD HEADQUARTERS—A CONSID-
ERABLE BENEFIT TO BOTH STUDENTS AND EMPLOYERS

the evening college and the judicious use of world class adjunct faculty from business and industry.

In this talk, I have but one "slide" and have chosen to substitute for that slide a faithful reproduction which is to be found at each place. It is a recent editorial from one of our local newspapers, the *Southfield Eccentric*. It briefly describes the long and mutually beneficial series of interactions between the city and the college. More particularly, it points out how student projects improve the already fine quality of life for the citizens of Southfield. It is this very same concept of fine quality of life to which our mayor, council, city administrator and other city officials are dedicated. One of the reasons our friend, the city treasurer, is smiling broadly is the fact that the college pumps more than $11 million per year into the local economy.

I have chosen the title *A Tale of Three Students* because there is something Dickensian about our students. As a general rule, they are not affluent and they have encountered personal circumstances which would deter them from getting an education if Lawrence Tech did not exist. It is at that point that we separate ourselves from Charles Dickens and provide an institutional environment which encourages their professional development and the enhancement of their talents.

Beverly Bercaw was a divorced woman with two small children when she entered Lawrence Tech in 1975. She graduated with a perfect 4.0 average accompanied by a degree in data processing and the presidential handshake. She holds the title of systems officer with Manufacturers Bank and, because Lawrence Tech was there when she needed it, she is also a dedicated adjunct faculty member in the evening college.

As we consider our historical approach to analyzing our continuing practices at this college, it is quite clear that we should continue to be dedicated to a class of students of enormous importance to the well-being of our society and for whom few institutions are designed to serve.

I started college with a scholarship to Kenyon College in Gambier, Ohio. The year was 1946. I finished Highland Park High School in June 1946 and entered Kenyon that summer. I encountered the most ferocious (and useful!) competition from those who entered on the GI Bill and who had had four or five years ripped out of their lives by

LIT DRAWS STUDENTS FROM NEARLY ALL STATES AND SIXTY NATIONS OVERSEAS. THE COLLEGE HAS GRADUATED 13,500 SINCE ITS FOUNDING IN 1932

World War II. These determined students would characteristically work all of the problems in the textbooks, get A's on all of the tests, etc.—exactly the kind of motivation and initiative I'm talking about tonight.

According to Stephan Sharf, who until recently was executive vice-president for manufacturing at Chrysler Corporation and has since been promoted to an even higher position: "As a general rule, I don't pay any attention to where my engineers have graduated but I do know which ones are from Lawrence Tech. They are the ones with enough guts and fire in the stomach who can be out in the plants, helping out on the floor. Lawrence Tech engineers are a shining example of that type of engineer." Steve is mentioned on page 76 of Lee Iacocca's book. (Favorably, I might add!)

Many students have stayed on campus just long enough to pick up the technical background they needed to perfect their inventions and start their businesses.

A perfect example of this is A. Alfred Taubman who spent some time on our campus as an architectural student before launching his now legendary career as a businessman. We regard him as a quick learner! We were pleased to award an Honorary Doctor of Architecture degree to Al Taubman at last Sunday's commencement. At the same ceremony, we bestowed an Honorary Doctor of Management degree upon Dr. Richard Lesher, president of the United States Chamber of Commerce and our Alumni Achievement Award to Charles Knighton, a graduate of the college who is vice president in charge of mid-size and small cars for the Ford Motor Company.

In his introduction, Dr. Gresham commented on the record of fiscal responsibility that this college exhibits. My three predecessors, Russell E. Lawrence, E. George Lawrence and Wayne H. Buell, understood the necessity for this with nearly excruciating clarity. Dr. Buell would repeatedly state that excellence follows from efficiency and not the other way around. Allow me to use the single example—of many possible— of the Lawrence Tech computer center.

It is my public statement that the nerve center of the campus resides in the president's office. In plain point of fact, its geographical placement might be more accurately considered to be in the computer center located across the street in the Science Building. We are leaders in computer-assisted engineering, architecture, management and science; additionally, I claim, in the application of the concept of the computer-assisted presidency!

If you visit our computer center, you will note that we have the finest modular furniture from Grand Rapids. This is because our treasurer and director of business affairs persuaded a very large and prestigious firm in Grand Rapids to provide a 58 percent discount. Surely, we would have settled for the next lower line of furniture. Ironically, that would have cost more than this special sale. Mel was alert to get us the best at a favorable price.

We have also the finest and most up-to-date hardware in computer equipment. We simply must. However, you will find during this hypothetical visit, a blue 380 MB Disk Drive for which our computer center director, John Grden, paid $15,000. One of our computer

LAWRENCE INSTITUTE OF TECHNOLOGY EMPHASIZES FAMILIARITY WITH THE COM-
PUTER AS ESSENTIAL IN ALL DISCIPLINES. ALL LIT STUDENTS HAVE PERSONAL "AC-
COUNTS" ON THE COLLEGE'S MAIN COMPUTER AND, IN ADDITION TO ACADEMIC WORK,
CAN USE THE COMPUTER TO COMMUNICATE WITH OTHER STUDENTS, FACULTY, AND
ADMINISTRATORS—INCLUDING THE PRESIDENT

vendors ordinarily takes these blue Control Data disk drives, paints them orange and charges $30,000. Shades of Caspar Weinberger and the $600 ash trays! As you will recall, he plans to use mayonnaise jars instead of ash trays. We too use the mayonnaise jar approach when appropriate; the trick is to know when to use jars and when to use state-of-the-art equipment.

A final anecdote on this subject concerns the spectacular new Digital Equipment Corporation (this is not the company mentioned a few minutes ago!) Operating System denoted 4.1. It has been a great advance; as far as we can tell, we were the first organization, bar none, in southeastern Michigan to implement this system fully and bring it on-line with no "glitches." The computer center crew volunteered to come in on their day off—April 8, 1985—so as not to disrupt the smooth utilization of the computer center by the students who were scheduled to return from Easter break on April 9. They put in a fifteen-hour day without any compensation on an entirely voluntary basis! *Esprit de corps* is one phrase to fit such a situation. We use the terms commitment and dedication. It is a commodity that cannot be bought.

How does this fiscal care and efficiency lead to excellence and community service? Consider our partnership with Henry Ford High School in the Detroit Public School system. The principal, Dr. Elijah Porter, is with us tonight. His academic background is in mathematics; hence, he is particularly aware of the needs of his fast-track students— dubbed Project Alpha—to have available to them the most appropriate computer equipment, robots, etc. Lawrence Tech seniors and juniors in engineering, architecture, science and management will serve as big brothers and sisters in this interaction which, in our view, is "where it's at" in higher education today.

One of our junior mechanical engineering students, Royal Bryson, is student coordinator of this project on behalf of Lawrence Tech. He is a former protégé of Dr. Porter, having been under his tutelage when Dr. Porter was at Renaissance High School. Royal, by the way, transferred to our college following a successful academic career at the University of Michigan.

Our careful practices allow us to develop the resources which permit the purchase of needed high technology equipment. The fact that we

CLOSE STUDENT AND FACULTY INTERACTION IS STRESSED AT LAWRENCE INSTITUTE OF TECHNOLOGY. "THEORY *AND* PRACTICE" IS THE COLLEGE MOTTO—THEREFORE, PRACTICALLY ALL FACULTY HAVE SUCCESSFUL INDUSTRIAL OR MANAGEMENT EXPERIENCE

have a compact campus housing three student bodies in one set of buildings is another LIT practice which conserves resources.

Will this account of how ideas are successfully turned into reality turn into a relentlessly unrelieved series of what might appear to be testimonials?

No, indeed! Let me mention the name of a graduate whose flair for individualism led him into what might be euphemistically termed

LAWRENCE INSTITUTE OF TECHNOLOGY'S NEWEST ACADEMIC BUILDING IS THE WAYNE
H. BUELL BUILDING, OPENED IN 1982

controversial aspects of entrepreneurialism. If I don't comment on this, I will surely be reminded of it during the question and answer period: John Z. Delorean.

One morning some years ago, I picked up my *Wall Street Journal* early in the morning to read an initial account of how the "coolly brilliant former GM engineer" had been charged with serious offenses.

Soon after, both the *Detroit News* and the *Detroit Free Press* called to ask me for my reaction.

With an inspiration born of the urgency of the situation, I replied that we graduated the "coolly brilliant former GM engineer" mentioned in the *Wall Street Journal*. All of his controversial behavior had been learned somewhere else!

Finally, will we accept students who wish to turn ideas into reality and who have progressed into college unimpeded by adversity? Of course we will. Let me introduce my son, Dennis Marburger, vice president of investments for the Bloomfield Hills Office of the Wall Street brokerage firm of Dean Witter Reynolds and my daughter, Kathryn Charles, who is a senior general accountant for General Motors Corporation. Both of them graduated from our School of Management; at most, the only personal situation they had to contend with was a tyrannical father.

On that rising note, I would like to thank you for your kind attention, express appreciation for a magnificent award and, in a spirit of good fellowship, happily offer to suspend the question and answer period.

Thank you and good night!

THE END

"Actorum Memores simul affectamus Agenda!"